MW01043554

To Leah, Happy 5th mom.
To the cutest baby
ever! 🌸 Love,
Erica
Andrews

AuthorHouse™
1663 Liberty Drive
Bloomington, IN 47403
www.authorhouse.com
Phone: 1 (800) 839-8640

© 2015 Erica Andrews. All rights reserved.

No part of this book may be reproduced, stored in a retrieval system, or transmitted by any means without the written permission of the author.

Published by AuthorHouse 1/31/2015

ISBN: 978-1-4969-6603-2 (sc)
ISBN: 978-1-4969-6604-9 (e)

Any people depicted in stock imagery provided by Thinkstock are models, and such images are being used for illustrative purposes only. Certain stock imagery © Thinkstock.

This book is printed on acid-free paper.

Because of the dynamic nature of the Internet, any web addresses or links contained in this book may have changed since publication and may no longer be valid. The views expressed in this work are solely those of the author and do not necessarily reflect the views of the publisher, and the publisher hereby disclaims any responsibility for them.

authorHOUSE®

Wildflowers Along the Wayside

A Tribute to Compound Words

By Erica Andrews

This book is dedicated to my mother and my daughter (my muse). Thank you "melancholy" for the thought melon cauliflower, melon cauliflowerpot, watermelon cauliflowerpot!

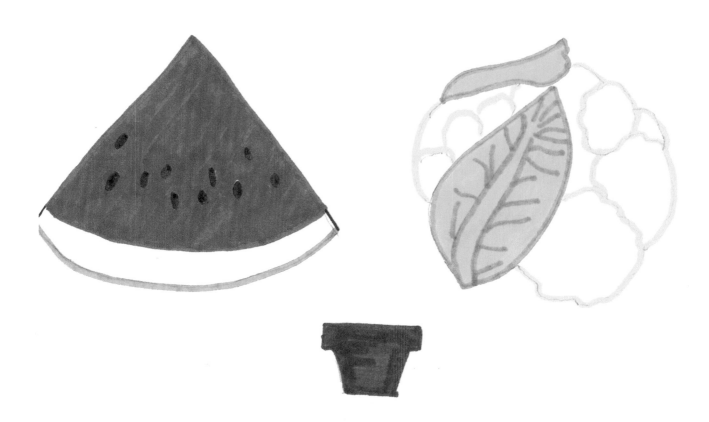

wildflower

flowerbed

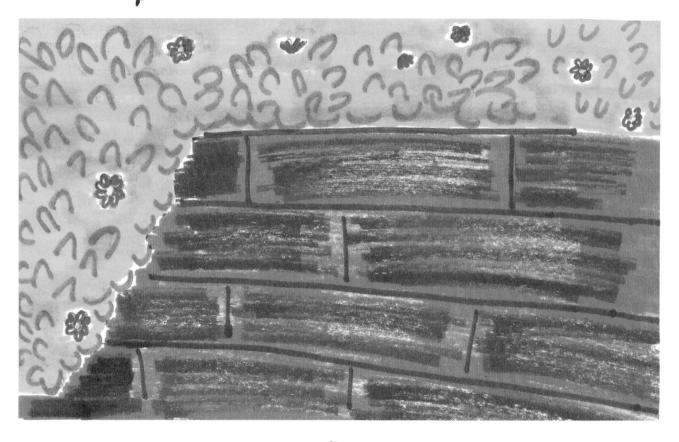

bedtime

timeline

2009 — I was born!
2010 — Got a dog!
2011 — First day of school!
2012 — Lost a tooth!
2014 — Learned to ride bike!

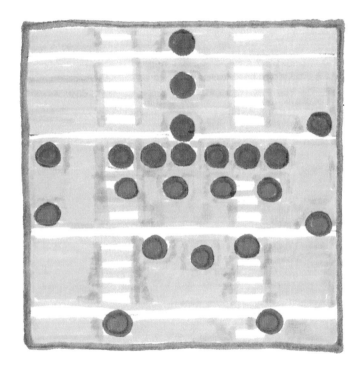

Lineup

uplift

liftoff

offspring

springtime

timetable

9:00	10:00	11:00	12:00	1:00	
Writing	Reading	Math	Lunch	Art	MON.
Reading	Math	Writing	Lunch	P.E.	TUES.
Math	Writing	Reading	Lunch	Library	WED.
Writing	Reading	Math	Lunch	P.E.	THURS.
Book Buddies	Writing	Math	Lunch	Music	FRI.

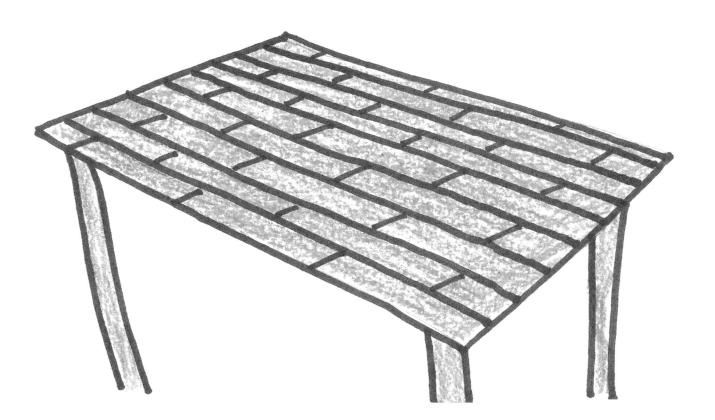

tabletop

topsail

12

sailboat

boathouse

housework

workout

outside

sidewalk

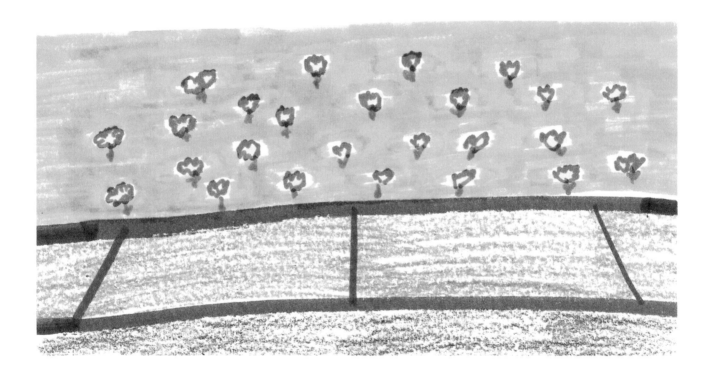

walkway

wayside